# Wicks

For Bill
and
Myra ?

from
Marie
and
Brian
and

Ben
Wicks.

*by Ben Wicks*

McClelland and Stewart

ISBN 0-7710-8995-3

McClelland and Stewart Limited
*The Canadian Publishers*
25 Hollinger Road
Toronto, Ontario
M4B 3G2

Printed and bound in
the United States of America

# INTRODUCTION

I have been asked to write an introduction to this book. Many might ask: "What kind of bleeding publishers would be so skimpy as to make the genius who has worn his fingers down to the bone suddenly take pen in hand and add even more pages to an otherwise sure best-seller?" The publishers approached various famous people in the hope that one or the other would agree to knock off a few well-chosen words in praise of this book. All wanted to do what they could, but for various reasons found themselves unable to find the words that would most aptly express the way they felt.

Therefore, it has been necessary to go outside the field a little in our search for comments. During the course of a working day I receive hundreds, nay thousands of compliments on my work. However, on approaching these fans, it was impossible to nail down one that would sign his or her name to a letter of endorsement. The people who have commented in their own inimitable way are in fact known only to their direct next of kin.

We don't need tripe of this kind. We consider this degrading and disgusting so are returning this copy of your cartoon...

A question for you, Sir. What Canadian in his right mind would pay money for your imbecilic, inane, inconsequential, snide, and, lastly, unsolicited comments on Canadian social habits? Such drivel can only lessen the newspaper's chances of gaining increased circulation.

A PROUD *CANADIAN*

What can be Ben Wicks' motive in his relentlessly recurring references to the private life of the Prime Minister? Mr. Wicks is a rare bird – a Cockney character without true humour or wit.

W. C.
OAKVILLE

I have fumed silently over Ben Wicks' attacks on our Prime Minister, but I shall remain quiet no longer. This is in poor taste, as are most of his snide and indelicate cartoons. Ben Wicks goes too far. Please have him clean up his act.

A. M.
ISLINGTON

And from a letter to the editor...

I think you have gone bananas to keep that scribbler
Ben Wicks on your payroll.

V. K.
TORONTO

To my mind, all of the above are complete
idiots and wouldn't know a bloody good
book if it fell on them.

Ben Wicks
Toronto, Ontario
Canada

To my wife, Doreen

Once upon a time a group of emi-
grants set out in search of a new land.
A violent storm sunk their ship and
tossed them onto the shore of a
far-a-way island.

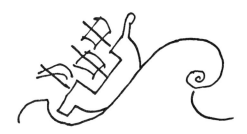

Quickly organizing themselves into a
civilized body they prayed for the day
that a ship would arrive and take
them to the Utopian country of their
dreams ... Canada.

A leader was chosen from the polit-
ically minded of the group. Someone
they could trust. A person who
promised them that help was on the
way and that their troubles
were over...

One Hundred and Twelve years later
another leader made the same
promises.

12

*"Jones, Smith, Brown, Lee, Harris..."*

"I managed to get the last tree."

"What makes you think you'd make a good Santa?"

'I will buy her a fur coat for Christmas...I will buy her a fur coat for Christmas...'

"I don't want anything for
Christmas, said the loving
son to his father who was
hard hit by inflation."

"If I could grant wishes
do you think I'd be
doing this stupid job."

"I've had Napoleons and Hitlers,
but I'll be honest
– this is a first."

'Would it make any difference if
I told you I was the real thing?'

"Don't talk to me
like that. I'm not
one of your elves!"

*'I hope they leave soon. We're down to the good scotch!'*

*'For goodness sake, Edith. It's supposed to look silly!'*

*"How was this week's Riot."*

*'I'm the hostage. Your husband will be down in a minute!'*

"Him? Oh he's the warden. The guys are holding him hostage."

'Who says crime doesn't pay?'

"Help! I'm being held hostage."

'Eleven!'

"Naturally my client beat the little old lady. It was a natural impulse at the frustration of finding her purse empty!"

23

**'I'll get you for this, Clark!'**

"I'm undecided. I still don't know which leader I hate the most."

'Just because I don't like him doesn't mean I don't want to see him.'

"Vote for me and I promise that you'll not hear from me again."

"What do you mean you're undecided?"

"Sure I'll vote for
you. Who is this?"

"It's okay dear. It's only
Ed. He got carried
away at our meeting and..."

'You're worrying too much about
Clark. A man who's younger...has
more hair...is better on TV...'

'Bye dear, have a nice day!'

30

*"Which day did you wish to travel?"*

*"I'm sorry We've run out of "get away from it all' places."*

*'Owing to an unforseen strike, passengers are asked to remain in the air until further notice.'*

*"Those half-fare passengers leaving us for Denver, please adjust your chutes."*

"What do you mean there's been a price hike on the route? I haven't told you where I'm going yet."

"We'd like two tickets to
a place where the natives
are not restless."

"Welcome aboard Economy
Airlines Flight 101."

'How does the Red Brigade
feel about middle-aged
North American tourists?'

"This is your captain
speaking. For those wishing
to adjust their watches,
it is exactly five minutes
to another fare increase."

"As my secretaries, have any of
you any ideas on how we can cut
government spending?"

"I'm determined to cut government
spending if I have to spend another
billion dollars doing it!"

'Government spending!
Government spending!
Government spending!'

'The dollar is falling!
The dollar is falling!'

*'Inflation, inflation, that's all
you ever think about!'*

*'The boat we mention,
Admiral, does not refer
to an aircraft carrier!'*

*"I'll be honest, Miss Brown. We
are not in the habit of making
bank loans for two chops
and a pound of sausages."*

*"How about a few thousand
to prop up my dollar?"*

*"We've decided to cut government spending and I'd like you to do your bit...by quitting!"*

*"I'll be honest. Your loan approval will not be easy seeing that you need the money."*

*'I knew there was something wrong when it showed the cost of living coming down!'*

*"There's been a security leak. The workers have found out we've increased our profits."*

44

*'Excuse me, sir. We're running out of fuel!'*

*'Hold it, you idiots! Don't you know there's an oil crisis?'*

*"Ten dollars for the fill up and a buck for the spare mouth full."*

*'Is it my fault we get stuck in an unsold car line-up?'*

"For the last time — I haven't got any gas!"

"It's our way of helping the overdeveloped countries."

"What's a line-up?"

'How about a souvenir model of
one of my oil well rigs?'

"Once again Americans found
themselves forced to line
up for gas today..."

"What on earth has being out
of gas got to do with the
car stopping, Johnson?"

'You can take your time.
We're out of gas!'

'With the fall in gold prices,
could you make it a silver?'

"I'm afraid the doctor is busy
with a gold filling."

"Buy Gold..."

"Good news, Mr Jenkins.
The gold you dropped
on your foot is up again."

"Oh, that's Mr. Lewis. He
has five gold fillings."

'And last, I'd like to thank
my mother.'

"They're here looking for work."

'Somehow it's different to what I had imagined!'

'We're out of water!'

"You never take me anywhere."

'Do we have to hide if Anita Bryant comes to town, Dad?'

"Chauvinist!"

'It's the obedience school. Fido has dropped out!'

'You're asking me how I feel about abortion?'

'Two minutes to kick-off and
you want to use the washroom?'

"It's tragic really. He was out jogging to improve his health and got hit by a truck!"

"If both teams want the ball so badly, why don't they play with two balls?"

"The doctor told him to quit smoking but he wouldn't listen."

"Is it my imagination or
is this news a summer repeat?"

"I'm sure that won't improve
the quality of the new
programs, dear!"

"No, Dolly Parton did not get
nominated for outstanding
actress in a supporting
role!"

"Do you have something that
will help me to get a man?
Preferably heterosexual."

**"Oh Harold, it's terrible. The doctor says Junior is going to grow up to be normal!"**

"Men love it. It smells
like a six pack."

'I don't care if she is wanted by
the Italian police. Sophia Loren
is not hiding out in my house!'

"Don't you want to stay and
watch the third quarter?"

"We're still married after
20 years. Where did we
go wrong?"

**"I don't understand it. Everyone seems to be separating."**

"The elves are demanding
a shorter work year."

"Speaking..."

"What did you bring me?"

"Just once I'd like the kids
to get a look at 'jolly old
Santa' at home."

"I'd like a washroom."

"And another thing — we're sick of you taking all the credit!"

'You never take me anywhere!'

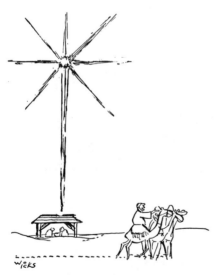

'That looks like a good spot to drill for oil!'

'Don't give me that 'ho, ho, ho' jazz. Where have you been?'

*So their leader found
them the promised land,
and they were happy…*

76

"Stop worrying about business
and watch the sun go down!"

'And I thought we had a
housing problem!'

'At the price of apples it's the
best we can do, Ma'am!'

'I'm not surprised he looks like that with today's prices.'

"And over here is our newest escape deterrent."

'It's safe to talk. The RCMP have checked the phone for bugs!'

'What a day! One hundred and fifty letters to open and we couldn't get the kettle to steam!'

'Come quick, everyone. Joe's found another bug!'

"Congratulations. It's a
feminist!"

"If you ask me, Dolly Parton's
fame is vastly overblown."

"I've been drafted!"

"One thing for sure.
She wasn't married."

'How much is it with the extras?'

"Don't laugh. With the grass catcher attached he still gets 298 miles to the gallon."

"I suppose if straw was $310 an ounce you'd make gold."

"Everyone I know bought gold!"

"It's the very latest model, runs on hay."

"Forget the straw into gold nonsense. Can you turn straw into yen?"

'And get this. It does 278 miles to the gallon on the highway!'

"With its revolutionary design it saves fuel by constantly moving downhill."

"Water!"

**'Get me the Prime Minister
and hurry!'**

"It's ...dis...grace..ful..
the..way..the press continue
to write...stories about..
Margaret Trudeau!"

"Wanna hear something funny?
It says here that marijuana
causes hallucinations, man!"

"If it's any help she was
reading a book on the life
of the Prime Minister of
Canada."

'I'm not much on the Middle
East. How are you on Margaret
Trudeau?'

14/6 ©TSS

IT'S THE ONE DAY OF THE YEAR I HATE —

17/6 ©TSS

HAPPY FATHER'S DAY !

HA HA HA HO OooO

Wicks

OH NO — CLARK !

22/6 ©TSS

FATHER KELLY. I HAVE SINNED —

— SO I SAID TO TRUDEAU — OH YEH. YOU AND WHO ELSE — THEN HE SAID...

BOR-ING

Wicks

91

"How about 'Unemployment', an ideal game for ages 18 to 25 years!"

"How do I know you're not the Ayotallah Khomeini?"

'You're late!'

"What seems to be the problem?"

"How come it uses so
little gas?"

"You want the premium
expensive or the regular
expensive?"

"Be on the lookout for a stolen
shopping cart. Two pounds of
sausages, three pounds of
potatoes, one steak..."

"And while it's true that our Lord never suffered the concerns of an oil crisis..."

"I thought there was an oil shortage."

"How come first we need oil then we don't?"

"May I recommend a vintage 1980 import."

"Excuse me, Sir. Jones claims
that he's found a new source
of energy."

*'I think this is what you had in mind. One bedroom, two bathrooms and three mortgages!'*

**"This is a real steal. It belonged to an oil shiek who couldn't keep up the payments."**

*"By the time I was your age I was worth 20 million dollars. And that's when 20 million dollars was worth something."*

*'I have bad news, eighty-nine. Your appeal has been turned down. You must return to high food prices and unemployment!'*

"Sorry I'm late. I was attending
a strike meeting."

"Does it say what time the next strike will be?"

'We knew he wasn't a mailman when we caught him delivering letters!'

"He's threatening to take our letters with him if we don't meet his demands."

"It's the ghost of Christmas past!"

"I had a terrible dream last night.
There was peace on earth and
goodwill towards men!"

"Okay. So we've got a 'club limitation pact', now what?"

"Limit arms as much as you like but if you really want peace you've got to fight for it."

'Who's the joker?'

'It seems that an arms manufacturer makes them in his spare time!'

"My husband and I just love
a good Newfie joke!"

"I'm telling you for the last time. I am not a boat person!"

'Quick, tell me. Did you see Prince Andrew and did he ask for a date?'

'OK I promise. If we don't like it, we'll leave early.'

"Wave your flag, dear. Here she comes!"

"Keep an eye on Olga. There's talk that she's thinking of defecting."

"He's really a bricklayer but it's the only way he can get out of Russia."

"In upholding your legal rights as a Soviet citizen, you have been granted a secret trial."

"You'll never guess who just defected."

*"Defections? Second door on the right!"*

'May I recommend a quart of 30 weight vintage Saudi Arabian?'

'Oh no. Not meat again!'

'You mean you want to be a human again?'

'I'll be frank. Not knowing who your mother and father are won't help in our search for your roots.'

115

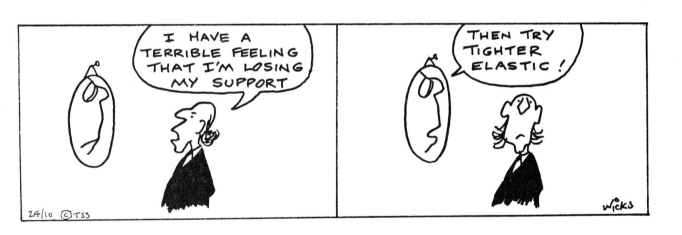

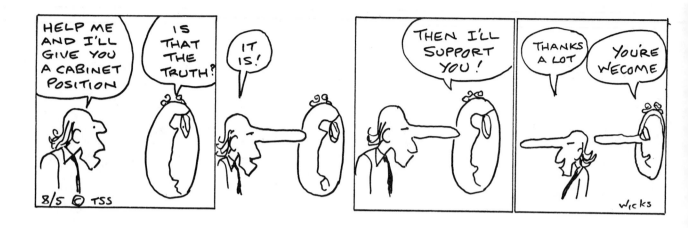

125

"I still think justice would have been better served if it had been for the deaf."

'Donny's getting married!'

'What's new with Princess Margaret?'

"You're too hard on yourself!"

"This, along with some bunker oil, will make them feel they're still in the sea."

"This is the IRA. We've got
Margaret Thatcher and either
we get what we want or we'll
send her back."

"Don't worry about it. We'll catch
it when it's recalled!"

"How do you spell IRA?"

"So you're with Chrysler. Look
on the bright side. If you'd
been with Edsel you'd have
been unemployed years ago."

"The Grand Wizard would like a
word with you!"

"Do you see John Travolta anywhere?"

"Good God. It's doing my job!"

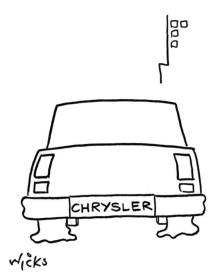

'You can't fire me, I quit!'

"Look on the bright side, Herbie.
If you weren't at school, you'd
be unemployed!"

"I asked if you'd pay me if I left, not if you'd pay me if I promised to leave!"

' Okay. One last thing before we get out there. Anyone want to go tinkles?''

"Which one is yours?"

"Happy Father's Day!"

"I'd like a sex change please!"

"So how come they're not smiling?"

"I've decided to ban smoking in the factory. Cigarettes, that is!"

'You smoke too much!'

'Where's your search warrant?'

"Smoking or non-smoking?"

138

"Whose idea was it to hang
mistletoe in the mess hall?"

"Hold it! I want an arms
limitation pact!"

'It's no good, you're still in
time. Try loosening the
strings a bit more!'

'It's a nice idea but it's been
done!'

"Is this what they call a
Petrocan, Dad?"

"And another thing. When it's time to 'kiss in' the New Year make sure I know where to find you."

"If you want to know what it's like being held a prisoner, ask me?"

"Don't let the Ayatollah catch you wearing lipstick!"

"Hitch up the camels
and form a circle"

"Lucky for you I'm not
the Ayatollah Khomeini."

"You're forgetting something.
Before we take hostages
we need an embassy."

"He just breathed on my wittle pawn!"

'Two pints! That should cover you for 1977, Mr. Stone!'

'Which wine country has the cleanest feet?'

"Gee Frank, I didn't know you cared!"

163

165

"Furthermore if elected
I promise to resign."

168

"He hasn't stopped since
they announced the
winner of the election."

"Dad's gone over to the old house to hang some new curtains."

"Hi. It's me again."

"Tell us what it was like before Trudeau."

"Even if you do find oil, we'll still be forced to hike the price of gas."

**'What time is the next fare increase?'**

*"Big deal! So you can make yourself invisible. So can Trudeau."*

*"Where do you want the new pool, Mr. Trudeau."*

*"I don't care if you prefer the old house. We're staying here and that's final."*

"Why should we?"

"Well, if it isn't Karol Jozef Wojtyla. What brings you back to Poland?"

"I'm sorry you were
disappointed, Miss Jones.
Maybe the Pope will drop
in next week."

"The plumber's here."

"Hush! Jane Fonda has
found a new cause."

'One thing's for sure. We
know it isn't swine flu!'

"If we can make friends with China, you can make friends with my mother!"

'As the victim of a rape, do you plead guilty or not guilty?'

"In order to counter criticism of NATO, I propose a change of name to NEATO!"

'I must confess, I love all God's creatures, but what's so important about getting the beetles together?'

"The referendum is coming..."

We had a separation referendum and voted "oui."

'He wants a Farrah Fawcett-Majors!'

'In all the years down here I've never known a winter like this one!'

"He needs cheering up. Tell him Trudeau's quit."

"It's days like this that
make me want to quit
now, instead of next week."

"You'll have to speak up. I'm a little deaf."

"It's Carter. I think he's crying."

"I've decided to give a press conference. Arrest some newsmen!"

"If God had meant us to get out of Afghanistan he wouldn't have sent us here in the first place."

"Don't bother to wrap it, I'll burn it here."

"Say please."

"Headquarters? Those people who invited us into their country are shooting at us. Over!"

"Sure we'll send in troops to help you...Who are you?"

"Good afternoon. I represent a group of peace loving citizens...."

"I have good news. An
unforseen happening has
made it possible to obtain
a large number of hitherto
reserved Olympic games
tickets."

"Don't you think that
bombing Moscow during
the Olympics will be
an over reaction?"

"I'll swap you two of my Dad
for one of Farrah-Fawcett."

"Remember what you did to
Lot's wife? Well there's
this guy Khomeini..."

"It's a Miss Piggy. She wants
you to know that she still
loves you."

187

"Morning Harry. What's new?"

**"This was made by baby Seals that died of old age."**

*'How many times have I told you not to bother me at the office, Doris?'*

**"My mother wants me to come home to Moscow. She has a non-refundable Olympic ticket."**

*"Crosbie may be impossible to understand, but I like what he says."*

"Then nasty old Pierre said "I'll huff and puff and I'll blow your house down.""

'It's our very latest. It destroys everyone but Arabs!'

"As far as I can make out, they've just had a visit from a guy called Stanfield."

'That reminds me. What time is supper?'

**'You'll never guess who's just left her husband!'**

"Chief! I picked up this
suspicious character in
a phone booth!"

'What is it now?'

'See, I told you snow tires were a waste of money!'

"What's this I hear about you wanting to join today's society Gregory?"

"How is it on gas?"

"How do I know you're not
Jane Fonda?"

'I'd like something for the
man who has everything,
including me!'

'I need a loan. Get me
the nearest Dentist!'

'What we need is a good war
'lest we forget!'

"Tell me again, Frank. Why
do we do this? I've forgotten."

'Now I know why fewer
people are watching television!'

*"Or how does "things go better with inflation grab you?"*

*"Despite a mass of hot air moving out of Ottawa, the forecast is for little change in all areas."*

*"All this talk of health plans makes me sick!"*

**'Don't just sit there. Get out and change the car!'**

"If John Travolta phones, tell him I'll be back in ten minutes!"

"It's our chauffeur. We're out of gas."

'It's the mailman! He has our letters and wants a ransom!'

'How be we give you a call when they start capital punishment again?'

**"Excuse me, ma'am, there's been a slight mishap. Our wheels have been recalled."**

'I may not be liberated, but I
know what I like!'

"All this talk about constitution.
When I was a boy we ate prunes.
That soon fixed it."

"Excuse me Captain. We have
an energy crisis. Eight
more rowers are dead."

"The computers have asked me
to represent them in the
upcoming wage negotiations."

'No wonder it's not filling up.
You've left the motor running!'

"I can give you a loan at prime, but I'll need proof that you don't need it."

"Can you really remember when mortgages were at 6% interest?"

'What you need is a job.'

**'Whatever gave you the idea that I was happy to see you go back to school?'**

*'Do you see a job anywhere?'*

*'I'm majoring in unemployment!'*

*"Sure I feel sorry for the boat people but is that any reason we should be discussing them while I'm eating?"*

*"Give me one good reason for saying 'No' to this little beauty."*

**"If I kiss you, will you change me into a frog?"**

"Two tickets to the
Olympics in Moscow."

"We could threaten them
with the sixth fleet,
if it wasn't already
there."

"If I'd known we'd be staying
in Afghanistan I'd have
never bought an Olympic
ticket."

'They find it easier to wail since
putting Carter's poster up on the wall.'

"Gas is up. Food is up. Your mother has died and Carter is still President!"

"We'd like two tickets to a place where the natives are not restless."

'Wow!'

"Well, how be we give
Reagan plus Kennedy
for the hostages."

"Hold it right there!"

"If I had known Khomeini was
going to get in I would never
have had the face-lift."

216

217

"Okay okay. yes I'll vote
for you. Cross my heart.
Now can I go back to bed?"

"Have you ever considered politics?"